Windows 10

The Ultimate Guide for Beginners to Operate Microsoft Windows 10

By Malcolm Schwartz

The information provided herein is stated to be truthful and consistent, in that any liability, in terms of inattention or otherwise, by any usage or abuse of any policies, processes, or directions contained within is the solitary and utter responsibility of the recipient reader. Under no circumstances will any legal responsibility or blame be held against the publisher for any reparation, damages, or monetary loss due to the information herein, either directly or indirectly.

Respective authors own all copyrights not held by the publisher.

Legal Notice:

This book is copyright protected. This is only for personal use. You cannot amend, distribute, sell, use, quote or paraphrase any part or the content within this book without the consent of the author or copyright owner. Legal action will be pursued if this is breached.

Disclaimer Notice:

Please note the information contained within this document is for educational and entertainment purposes only. Every attempt has been made to provide accurate, up to date and reliable complete information. No warranties of any kind are expressed or implied. Readers acknowledge that the author is not engaging in the rendering of legal, financial, medical or professional advice.

Table of Contents

Chapter 1: An Introduction to Windows 10

Today, the big players in the computer industry like Google and Apple just give away the operating systems, this has put a damper on how Microsoft has conducted business for as long as we got to know and love the company. For this operating system, Microsoft decided to give it away between the dates of July 29th, 2015 all the way to July, 29th of 2016. Their hopes are that those with a licensed copy of Windows 7 or 8 will upgrade their computer to the newest of operating systems.

The reason behind their bit of change of heart is due to the issues that many have had in the past with having different Windows operating systems. With Windows 10 being the main operating systems as far as Windows goes, it is much easier for app designers to create apps that will work for more people. Before there were many people who had issues because an app may only be used by Windows 8 or 7, now, with the Windows 10 being free for that time period to download and upgrade, there is a larger mass of those that own devices to be able to utilize the applications that are created. Windows 10 is not the standard for Windows based computers.

Some may think that due to the past marketing, Windows will not be able to make money by offering the operating system for free for a year. However, this may seem true by just skimming the surface of their financial plan; digging a little deeper will tell you otherwise. Although they are giving up potential dollars by offering it for free; they are able to design the apps for many, many more people to utilize, and thus recouping their losses on the operating systems. Yes, this benefits the company, but also the users. If you have had past Windows, then you are well aware of the issues that can come up with software only being available for a specific version of Windows. So, everyone benefits.

If you are thinking about the succession of the version of Windows, you might have wondered why there was no Windows 9 released. True be told, there was never a Microsoft Windows 9. They skipped the number 9 and went straight to 10. The reasoning behind this is that the developers and the company believes that this specific operating system deserves more than a 10. In their words, Windows 10 is a "perfect 10".

Minimum Hardware Requirements

Microsoft has always been very great at ensuring that the lower end computers are able to run their system. This is no exception. Windows 10 has much of the same system requirements for Windows 8. If you need to know the specifications of Windows 10, here they are in the simplest of forms:

- **Latest OS**: Ensure that you are running the latest version of Windows - 7, SP1, or 8.1. Make sure that you update to one of those in order to update to Windows 10.
- **Processor**: 1 GB for 32 Bit or 2 GB for 64 Bit
- **RAM**: 1 GB for 32 Bit or 2 GB for 64 Bit
- **Hard Disk Space**: 16 GB for 32 Bit OS and 20 GB for 64 Bit OS
- **Graphics Card**: DirectX 9 or Later with WDDM
  1. 0 Driver
- **Display**: 800 X 600

Important Notes about Windows 10

In this section you will learn about some of the special notes that every Windows 10 user should know.

- Those who have Windows 10 Home Edition will automatically get updates through the Windows Update when the updates become available. Windows 20 Enterprise and Pro users will have an ability to postpone the updates. The amount of the time they can be postponed is limited.
- Smaller storage devices like the devices that have 32 GB hard drives or the older devices with a full hard drive may need some additional storage in order to complete the upgrade. You will see instructions that will tell you what you should do while it is upgrading. You need to either insert your USB flash drive or you will need to remove unneeded files for the computer.

- In order to perform an upgrade the computer will need to be connected to the internet. Windows 10 is a bigger file; about 3 gbs.
- To upgrade the device, the factors will go beyond the specifications. This will include the firmware and the driver support, feature support, and the application compatibility. This will be regardless of whether the device meets the system specifications of not for Windows 10.

Logging into Windows 10

There are three different ways that you are able to log into Windows 10. The three are using a PIN, password, or a picture password. From the login screen, you will be able to switch between the choices of logging into your computer.

In addition to the traditional password logon, Windows 10 has included a picture password and a PIN logon for your safety and the security of the other users. You are able to use Microsoft email accounts to logon or even a local account in order to gain access to your computer. However, there are some conflicts in design that may not allow you to use the picture password or PIN. For example, when you are in Safe Mode, neither of these ways will work and you will have to use the traditional way of logging in using a password. Here are the ways that you can set your login options.

- **Changing Password**: You are able to change your password by going to the Start Menu. Click on the Setting. Select Accounts. Next, you will choose Sign In Option. Hit the button that says Change underneath the Password heading. You will then enter your Current Password. Click on the Next button. You will then be prompted to enter a new password and a hint for your new password. Click on the Finish button.
- **Picture Password**: This will enable you to use a certain picture from the library as your password. You have to use three gestures on the picture that you want to use as the password. For example, you are able to select, draw, and even resize a portion of your picture that you would want. Under the settings application, under the option Picture Password. Click on the Add button. You will type in the user password, and then click OK in order to confirm the account information. Draw three gestures on your picture. Repeat this step and then click on the Finish button in order to exit.
- **PIN**: If you do not want to set up a Picture Password, then you are able to use a PIN in order to log into your computer. Go under Settings and then click on Accounts. Click on the Sin In Options. Select the change button under the PIN section. Enter your password, and then click on the OK button. Next, you will enter a new PIN. Click on Finish.

File Explorer in Windows 10

The File Explorer used to be known as Windows Explorer. It is the way you can get into your computer, whether you are looking for files, settings, or peripherals. This is often where you will begin the search. Windows 10 offers a new look to the interface of the File Explorer, and here is how you can tweak it.

First of all, you are able to customize the Quick access pane that offers important locations, recent files, and recent folders. You will right click on any of the frequent folder to get access to the options. Using your navigation bar that is on the left, you will click and then drag any entry in order to change its order in a queue and to get the most used folders first.

If you do not like Quick access and you would rather start up File Explorer with the old view instead, right click on the Quick access heading on the left side, choose the options, and then select This PC from the menu located at the top.

Chapter 2: How to Uninstall and Reinstall Windows 10 Built In Apps

The applications that are built into Windows 10 are pretty great; however, there are many, many alternatives that are available. You may want to delete one or more apps because you found an alternative that works better for you personally. Do not fret, there is a way that you can uninstall the apps and reinstall them should you want them back.

Uninstalling Windows 10 Built In Applications

Some of the default applications will allow you to manually uninstall them as you would another program or application, while there are others that will need a bit more effort. You will need to use the PowerShell in order to uninstall those that need more effort, as well as for those that you can uninstall in a traditional way.

- To uninstall an app in the traditional way, **right click** on your app and then you will select uninstall.
- For those that you need to use PowerShell for, type PowerShell into your Search Windows box. You must be logged on as the Administrator. Type in **'Get-AppxPackage*AppName*** | **Remove-AppxPackage'**. Change the 'AppName for your specific application name that you would like to remove.

You might want to check the name of the app before you try to delete it. For example, if you want to delete the weather app, the name is different. It is actually 'bingweather'. So, ensuring that you know the proper name of the app will ensure that you can delete it.

Reinstalling Windows 10 Built In Applications

In order to reinstall your default applications in Windows 10, you will need just one of the command. It will refresh all of your apps and then replace the ones that were removed when you were getting rid of some.

- Type in 'PowerShell' into your Search Windows box and then you will open it as the administrator.
- Type in **'Get-AppxPackage | Foreach {AddAppxPackage-DisableDevelopmentMode-Register "$($_.InstallLocation)\AppXManifest.xml "'.**
- You will then wait for the process to be completed.

Depending on the computer system, this process can take a bit longer. You may not be able to see the results either until you check the Start Menus and see your applications being returned.

Chapter 3: Fixing Display and Sound Issues in Windows 10

Just like other operating systems, there may be issues that can arise with the sound or the display. In this chapter you are going to learn how to fix the issues that can happen with your own computer using Windows 10. There are bugs that can happen, but is fixable with the information in this chapter.

Fixing Your Sound

In this section you are going to learn the steps that you need to perform in order to fix issues with your sound, or when there is no sound at all.

- You will right click on the sound icon that is located in the taskbar. It is at the bottom of your screen.
- Select the option Playback Devices from your menu.
- Choose your current playback device and then double click on it in order to open the properties.
- Go to the Advance tab and then change the bitrate to 24 bit / 44100 Hz or 24 bit / 192000 Hz, which will depend on the speaker configuration.

After you have done this, check to see if you still have sound issues. If you are still having an issue, restore the sound to fix the issue.

- GO to your Start Menu. Search for the Device Manager.
- Expand out the Sound and Audio Devices.
- Right click on the sound driver, then you will choose uninstall.
- Click on the option Scan for Hardware Changes.

- Updated drivers will be automatically installed to your computer.

Fixing Your Display

Microsoft has designed and released the Microsoft Automated Troubleshooting Service, also known as ATS Fix It. It will allow you to detect and fix issues automatically that mess with your display quality and the text readability. Once you have downloaded the ATS Fix It and ran it, it will scan for the issues. You are able to choose to allow it to fix all the problems automatically or you can opt to select and then apply the fixes manually. Once the scan is complete, it will then present you will the report.

You will click on the option Next in order to fix all the issues. Once the issues are fixed, it will show a list down and inform you of the issues that has been fixes with your computer. Once the troubleshooting has been completed, and you have fixed the issues, you are able to restart your computer.

Chapter 4: How to Secure Windows 10 Systems

With every computer, there is an owner that would like to ensure that their computer is safe. Having a Windows 10 computer is no exception. In this chapter you are going to learn about the security features that this operating system has to offer. Biometric authentication and application vetting headline the security features of Windows 10.

Marc Maiffret, Windows security experts expressed that with Windows 10 security features with the combination of the Windows Store for authorized, as well as vetted application, Microsoft has made the desktop ecosystem looks more like a smartphone, which is great for security.

Device Guard

Microsoft's Device Guard is has aimed at blocking the zero day attacks by vetting the applications that will try to access the Windows 10 machine, as well as the network. It blocks any application that is not signed by certain software vendors, the enterprise itself, and the Windows app store.

Fujitsu, Acer, NCR, HP, Par, Lenovo, and Toshiba has teamed up with the company Microsoft to use the Device Guard on their devices that are Windows based.
It supports a point of sale system, ATM, and even other internet devices that run Windows.

In order to help protect the users from malware, once an app is executed, the program will make a determination on if the app is trustworthy, and it will notify the user if it is not. The Device Guard can use virtualization and hardware technology in order to isolate that decision making the function from the rest of the operating system, which will help provide addition protection from malware or attackers.

Privacy Settings

You are able to access the privacy settings using the Control Panel, which is titled Setting in this certain operating system. The fastest way that you can get there is by using the keyboard shortcut; Windows-I. Another method to get there is to tap your Windows key, which will open the Start menu, and then you will click the Settings button. You are also able to right click the button and then select Pin to Taskbar in order to create a shortcut for you to use later.

We will focus on the second to the last section in the Settings, which is labeled Privacy. Sine your Settings tool will bring you back to wherever you had left off, you may not see your Privacy button if you have been messing with the Settings. If that is the case, then you will click the back arrow in the left hand upper corner of your window to go to the home page.

Before you start messing with everything, here is a word of warning; although you have tempted to disable everything that will reduce the privacy, doing so may disable or impair some apps and the interactions between certain aps. If you find that this is an issue, you will have to come back and then re-enable things until the issue goes away. This can be a bit time consuming if you have made a lot of changes. Unfortunately, the Privacy section will not have a button to restore your default settings, so you will have to track the changes that you have made. It is recommended that you take screenshots of the sections before you make any changes.

General Pane

Clicking on your Privacy button will open a window that has two panes. On the left is your category list, and then on the right is the settings for the categories that you are looking at. In the General pane, there are settings listed. These are SmartScreen, advertising ID, and language.

Advertising ID identifies the Web behavior to deliver certain ads. If wikis in this manner: if you open your Windows 10 Travel app and also your Calendar app, Microsoft is able to use that information in order to show you certain ads. That is assuming that the app uses ads. You will not begin seeing banner ads when you open your calculator, but Microsoft Edge can run these certain ads once you go to Outlook.com or Bing. However, it does not offer any personal information to the company about you. It is a bit like a beacon in order to deliver ads that are relevant to you so that you are more likely to click on them. It is to give you a better shopping experience.

The SmartScreen is a filter and is a layer that Internet Explorer and Microsoft Edge uses in order to help protect the computer from suspicious or dangerous websites. This filter does this in two different ways. One is that it analyzes the websites for any questionable behaviors like trying to open pop ups that are fake or redirecting you to another website. The second way is that it checks the address against a list that is maintained, which is a list of fraudulent sites. You will get a false positive once in awhile, but for the main part of surfing the net, you will be save and it is recommended that it is left on. The language setting will help websites detect what language that you are using so that they are able to deliver the language that you prefer.

Location Pane

If you are using the administrator account, then you will be able to see the option to disable the location information for all of the users on that specific device. Below that is the toggle that you can use for the specific account that is logged in, which will look grayed out if your location services are being disabled for everyone.

Location can be used in order to let Windows 10 apps to display region specific information like sports scores and weather, or to show map locations and even shopping choices in your specific area. If you disable the setting, you are still able to enter the location information in manually, id just will not be sent to you automatically.

There are some apps that will use the device's Bluetooth or the Wi-Fi functions in order to determine the location even when the location setting is not being used. You are able to toggle that feature on and off in your Radios pane. Bluetooth and Wi-Fi will still be able to function, just without the location information.

Camera and Microphone

As you have probably guessed, these sections include a toggle that will disable the webcam and your mic. You are also able to toggle certain apps, including the apps that are pre-installed and designed by Microsoft and the apps that you have also installed to replace these. If you have purchased the device from a builder like Acer, Dell, Lenovo, or Toshiba, they may even have some pre-installed apps too.

By default, Windows 10 apps get permissions for the camera and the mic regardless if you are going to use it, so it is recommended that you check the settings here and there if you are leaving the camera enabled. Typically, you should only give the camera and the mic access when you know that you will be using the app, like HipChat or Skype. Note that disabling the camera and the mic in your Settings may not prevent the malware from secretly enabling it again, and it will not have any effect on the operating system that you may be using to dual boot. You may want to put a piece of tape or something to that effect over your camera when you are not using it.

Inking, Speech, and Typing

The speech section is where you are able to toggle Cortana's speech recognition, among some other things. Cortana is like the loved Apple's Siri. However, it works on your desktop, as well as on the mobile devices. You are able to use the speech recognition in order to dictate your emails and more. Enabling this setting also improves other settings.

http://www.darkreading.com/cloud/microsoftwindows-10-three-security-features-to-knowabout/d/d-id/1320650
http://download.cnet.com/blog/download-blog/aguide-to-windows-10-security-settings/
http://download.cnet.com/blog/downloadblog/windows-10-privacy-settings/

Chapter 5: How to Use the Registry Editor to Manage Hardware and Software Issues in Windows 10

Windows Registry is deemed a hierarchical database that offers the entire configuration and the settings that is used by series, components, applications, and most of everything on the system. The registry has two main concepts that you should know. They are Values and Keys. The Values are somewhat like files inside of a folder, and they offer actual settings. Registry Keys are the objects that are folder, and in your interface it looks like actual folders.

When you open up your Registry Editor, you will see a tree type view on the left side of the pane and it will contain all of your keys, with values on your right side. It is about as simple as it can get.

The root level keys that you are seeing on the left side are very important. Each one will house different sets of information, so you will need to know which of the sections that you need to go into. The interesting thing that people do not know about is that there are three of the five items on this root level are not actually there, they are linked to the items further down in one of the keys.

HKEY_CLASSES_ROOT
Windows uses this specific section in order to manage file type association, and it typically abbreviated HKCR when being references in a document. This key is actually a link that is to HKLM\Software\Classes.

HKEY_CURRENT_USER

This holds the user settings for certain logged in users, and it is normally abbreviated HKCU. This is really linked to HKEY_USERS\<SID-FOR-CURRENT-USER>. The crucial sub key in this section is HKCU\Software, which has the user level settings for most of the software.

HKEY_LOCAL_MACHINE

All of your system wide settings are here, and it is normally abbreviated as HKLM. You will use the HKLM\Software key mostly in order to check the machine wide settings.

HKEY_USERS

Stores all of your settings for the users on the system. You will normally use HKCU instead; however, if you want to check the settings for another user on the computer, you are able to use this one.

HKEY_CURRENT_CONFIG

This stores all of your information about the current configuration of the hardware. This one is not used often, and it is a link to HKLM\SYSTEM\CurrentControlSet\Hardware Profiles\Current.

Creating New Values and Keys

If you right click on any of the keys in the left side of your window and will give you options, most of them are pretty straightforward and very easy to understand. You are able to create a new Key, which will then show up as a folder on the left side, or a new value, which will be on the right side. Those values are a bit confusing. However, there are only a couple of the values that you will use regularly.

- String value - REG_SZ: This has anything that will fit into a string. Much of the time, you are able to edit the human readable strings without breaking something.
- Binary Value - REG_BINARY: This value has arbitrary binary data, and you will probably never edit this one.
- DWORD - 32 bit, Value - REG_DWORD: These are always used for the regular integer value, no matter if it is a 0 or 1, or even a number from 0 all the way up to 4, 294, 967, 295.
- QWORD 64 bit, Value - REG_QWORD: These are not used most of the time for any registry hacking, but it is basically a 64 bit integer value.
- Multi-String Value - REG_MULTI_SZ: These are the values that are fairly uncommon however, it works like a notepad in a window. You are able to type multi-line textual information into a field.
- Expandable String Value - REG_EXPAND_SZ: These are the variables that have a string that is able to contain environment variables and often times is used for the system paths. A string may be %SystemDrive%\Windows and will expand to C:\Windows. This will mean that once you find a value in the Registry that is this type, you are

able to insert or change the environment variable and they will then expand before the string is used.

Favorites Menu

One of the most useful features that no one seems to even notice is the Favorites menu, which is wonderful when you want to check a location of a registry regularly. What is even more great than that is that you are able to export the list of the favorites and then use it again on a different computer without having to browse the keys and then add them to the menu. It is also a nice way to bookmark something that is in the registry if you want to look around in many different location, so you are able to easily flip back to the last one your were at.

Exporting Registry Files

You are able to export registry keys and all of your values contained under them by right clicking on the key and then choosing Export. This is important if you are getting ready to making any changes to the system. Once you have gotten the exported registry file, you are able to double click on it in order to enter the information back into your registry, or you are able to choose Edit to use Notepad to look at the contents.

Setting Permissions

Some of your registry keys will not allow you to make any changes by default. This is typically because you do not have any permissions to those keys; however, you are able to tweak the permission if you want just by right clicking on the key and then choosing Permissions, and then you need to adjust them from there.

Loading Registry Hives

You are able to use the path File, then Load Hive feature to load up a specific registry from another system. Perhaps you need to troubleshoot another system, and you would like to see what is going on in your registry for the system that is not booting. So you will boot the system from your rescue dick, or maybe using a Linux live CD, and then you will copy your registry files onto the thumb drive. Now you are able to open up a computer in order to look around by using the Load Hive feature.

Chapter 6: Installation Options for Windows 10

In this chapter you are going to learn how to install Windows 10 and the options that you will have. Before you do something to your computer, the rule of thumb is to back it up. Ensure that all of your data is backed up. There are three different ways that you can get Windows 10. You can purchase a newer PC with it preloaded, purchase a licensed copy online, or by upgrading your existing computer.

When you go to install this operating system, you will see a greeting that says, "Get going fast... change these at any time". However, it is highly suggested that if you care about your privacy, you will need to customize it, and choose not to go fast.

- **Personalization**: This will personalize your typing, speech, and inking input by sending the contacts and the calendar details along with other input data to the company Microsoft. Sent inking and typing data to Microsoft to improve upon the recognition and the suggestion platform It will let apps use the advertising ID for across apps. Location is on due to default unless you manually change it.
- **Browser and Protection**: SmartScreen online will help protect you against the malicious content and any download in the websites that are loaded by Windows Store apps and browsers. Use the page prediction in order to improve the reading, speed up your browser, and make the overall experience better in the browser. The browsing data will be sent to the company.
- **Connectivity and Error Reporting**: The computer will automatically connect to the suggested hotspots, even though all of the networks are not secure. It will also automatically connect to any shared networks that are on your contacts. It will send errors and diagnostic information to the company.

- **Applications**: On this screen you will choose the default apps that you would have to accept if you did the fast install. Here you are able to choose the applications that you actually want.

Chapter 7: How to Upgrade to Windows 10

In this chapter you will learn how to upgrade your computer to Windows 10. Just because it is an easy process, it does not meant that there are not things that you need to do before you go upgrading and the important choices to make while you upgrading. While there are many websites that point a person to the installer and telling them that they just need to download it and run it, you should take the time in order to give you a chance to use these tips.

What You Need
In order to upgrade your computer from Windows 7 or Windows 8 up to Windows 10, there is a very small list of things that you must have and a few that are recommended. Here is what you are going to need before moving ahead and then some of the best practices highlighted.
- **Activated Copy of Windows 10**: The most important aspect of this is the current version of Windows is activated properly. Although Microsoft has alluded to the idea that this

operating system would be a large sweeping upgrade that would install on even a pirated copy of Windows that plan never really came to pass and you need to have an activated copy. In order to check if the copy is activated, press the Windows Key + W in order to pull up your Setting search and then type in Activated in order to access the "See if Windows is Activated" menu. You can also look under the Control Panel, System in order to see your status.

- **Appropriate Windows 10 Update Tool**: ALthough the update tool is straight forward, you will need to right version for the hardware. The first step is to determine if you are running a 32 bit or 64 bit machine. You are able to check what version you are running by looking in the same panel as the activated panel above.

- **Running Upgrade Installer**: You will first be prompted to upgrade your computer or create an installation media for another computer. Select the option 'Upgrade this PC now' in order to begin your upgrading process. Click the Next button. This will begin the download process, which is short or long depending on your connection to the internet. When it is finished download and also unpacking the installation media you will be prompted to accept the terms of your new license agreement. You will need to click 'Accept' and then the installer will do an update check before moving over to a confirmation page.

By default, the installer selects the largest selection of 'what to keep'. If you would like to make changes to what you are keeping, click the small button 'change what to keep'. You will be prompted to select what type of installation you would like.

When you are ready, click on the Next button in order to proceed and then it will return you to final screen. Confirm that you are ready to go and it will show what you would like. After confirming your installation, click the Install page. The PC will then reboot a few times as your installer works and when it is done you will be returned to the login screen.

Configure Windows After Upgrade

When you get to the login screen for the first time, you are not done yet. There are some little tweaks that you can do before you boot into Windows. You should take advantage of them. As soon as you have logged in for the very first time you will be prompted to choose between Customize settings or Express Settings. You need to click on ' Customize Settings in order to see what has been set to default and confirm if you want them or not.

Chapter 8: Windows 10 Configuration to Protect Privacy

Everyone needs to protect private data. Whether you are carrying sensitive files for work, passwords, or sensitive pictures, there is specific information that you do not want anyone else to have. When you are setting up the computer, you are establishing habits that you are going to use through the time of the computer. Rather than waiting to care about the privacy settings later, it is better to do it now.

Before doing anything to your computer, you need to make sure that you are starting from a clean slate. If you have purchased your computer from the store, it probably came with a lot of software that is junk. Get rid of the junk in order to keep your computer running smooth. There is also software that can be intrusive.

- Wipe the computer and reinstall your operating system from scratch. This is one way to ensure that there is no extra junk on your system. If you have built your own computer, you are probably okay with this. If you are running a bought system, be sure to keep track of your license key before you do this.
- Remove any bloatware manually. It is a bit more of a process that is tedious, and it is possible to accidentally leave items behind, but it will allow you to clean your system without wiping it out completely.

A clean install is a great step in order to take regardless of if you are concerned about privacy or not. However, to make sure that there is nothing on the system that makes your data vulbernalbe, it is even more crucial. The only way to do this and be sure is to clear out everything when you first set up the computer.

Audit Your Privacy Section of Settings App

With the operating system Windows 8, Microsoft introduced the new style of apps. To go with this, Microsoft has also added a new system for permissions. This is geared towards tablets and phones, but as this company steers developers towards their store, there are more apps that are more likely to use the permissions in order to access things like the microphone, camera, or your location. In order to manage this permission, you will need to open the Start menus and type in 'privacy', and then choose the Privacy Settings. Here are the settings that you should tweak:

- **Location**: You are able to set your location that all of the apps will use, or you can disable the location tracking completely. You are also able to see a list of the apps that have the ability to use the location and disable or enable them per app.
- **Camera and Microphone**: You are able to block any access to the camera or your microphone per app, or you can disable the access completely. Just like the location settings, this section only will apply in the modern app

style. It also will not disable any devices on the system level.

- **Calendar, Contacts, and Messages**: If you are using any services from Microsoft that manages your events, contacts, or your messages, you are able to control which of the apps has access to the data.

- **Typing and Speech**: Under this you are able to disable the "get to know me" feature. This setting is placed a bit weird and it is unclear how much data is tracked with this one, but it does say that it is used to offer better suggestions, improve your dictation, and will help Cortana to get to know you. So, if you are not comfortable with this digital assistant learning your specific habits, it might be best to just turn it off.

Depending on how much you want the operating system to know about you specifically, it will be worth going through the Privacy section. Also, you need to keep in mind that any of the permission you will disable here only apply to your apps that are displayed. Microsoft's permission system is a bit new, so unless you have downloaded an app from the store, this probably will not prevent them from actually using your hardware.

Chapter 9: Guide to Windows 10 Backup

Once you have installed Windows 10 onto your computer, and you have installed all of the drivers that you need, as well as configuring your settings; the next step is to back up your computer and all of the settings. You are able to do this by creating an image backup of the system drive and storing it on a different partition on your local hard drive, a network location, or even a DVD. If anything ever goes wrong with your computer while you are working with it, you are able to revert right back to the previous state in just minutes. Here is how you will back up your computer:

- Log onto your computer through the administrator account.
- Once you have arrived to the desktop, right click on your Start button.
- From this menu, click on the Control Panel.
- In the Control Panel window, you will need to ensure you click 'View by' type is set on Category.
- Click on the 'System and Security' category, and then from this window, click on Security and Maintenance.
- From the bottom of the pane on the left, click on the File History link.
- Again, from the bottom of the pane to the left, click on System Image Backup.

- On this opened Create a System Image window, from the available buttons representing the corresponding options.
- Select the way you would like to save the backup file.
- Once you have selected the location, follow your on screen instruction in order to create the image backup.

Chapter 10: Restore and Recovery

You have upgraded to the Windows 10 operating system. But once you have made your change, you will want to ensure that you are able to backup and restore the data fast and conveniently. The Factory Reset and System Restore has been included into Windows 10, and are much better than they were with the operating system Windows 8.

No Recovery Partition

Microsoft is extremely confident in the refresh, restore, and reset tools that they have packaged into this version of Windows that there isn't a recovery partition. Whereas in the operating system Windows 8 you were able to use the recovery image on a hidden partition in order to restore the system, this is no longer an option. The reason behind this is to allow the user to maximize on the available disk space, which in conjunction with this file compression will save more than 6 GB on a 64 bit system that is running Windows 10. This will offer a large advantage to those will a small capacity of system.

As the partition was the nearest to having the installation media, this is not ideal. However, the refresh and the reset tools should be good enough to deal with any major issues, as long as you are making the right decisions between refreshing and restoring Windows.

Using the System Restore

If you are having problems with Windows 10's performance, the very first thing that you should look at is the list of the restore points. If one of these points coincides with the point in which the system began to misbehave, then you are able to use the System Restore tool in order to reinstate the setting and the software that were in place during this time.

You will need to open Start, then settings. You will then search the box type with create a restore point. Click on the matching result, select your drive that you would like to use in order to use for your restore point. Click on Configure, then Turn on System Protection. This action will activate the system restore functionality. Click on the OK button to confirm your choice, and then in the main window you will click on Create. This will create a restore point and you will then give it a name.

The system protection software will then create a restore point, which you are able to revert to later should you need to. You might need to spend just a few moments checking through the items that will be affected so that you are able to reinstall any software and avoid any apps that may have caused the issues.

Refresh a Windows 10 Computer

If reverting to a restore point did not resolve the issues with the computer, then you will need to refresh the setting. This will revert the system to a similar state to what it was when you had bought the computer. The only difference is that you be able to keep your data and your settings.

Open up Start, then Settings; once there you will click on Update & Security in order to begin. Select Recovery in the left menu. Under the 'Reset this PC', you will click or tap 'Get Started. You will then use the Keep my Files option. A warning will be shown, and a second might appear if you have upgraded to this operating system.

Reset Windows 10

There may come a time when you have to completely set your computer back to all of its original settings. This is much like a tablet or a smartphone. This action will restore the system to factory settings and it will leave it like new. You will need to backup any data that you need to keep.

You will need to go back to the Reset this PC option, and then click on Get Started. This time, you will not keep your files, you will select the option Remove Everything. Here you will have two different options; Just Remove My Files for quick reset and Remove Files and Clean Drive. The last option will take much longer, but it is the most secure; therefore, making it more useful for wiping your system clean before you sell it or give it away.

Chapter 11: Security of the New Windows 10

With good protection at the core, Windows 10 is by far the most secure of Windows ever. From the virtualization based security all the way to Windows Hello and Enterprise Data Protection, this operating system has concentrated on security, along with other modern features. Most of the issues that you hear other computer owners expressing concern for is covered by Windows 10 automatically by default. This operating system has many new features that have your security in mind.

Virtualization Based Security

You cannot talk about the security of this operating system without discussing the large, underlying security architecture that has been added known as the virtualization based security, also known as VBS. VBS uses certain software and hardware enforced mechanisms in order to create an isolated, hypervisor restricted, securing, specialized subsystem for storing, transferring, and operating other very sensitive subsystems and data.

VBS makes it extremely hard for any attacker to mess with the core components of your operating system. VBS is not just an improved defense, it represents the entire architectural change that largely reduces the surface area of attack and attempt to eliminate any attack vector. All malware and hacking will not just magically go away, but the VBS will create a secure environment where the parts of the operating system is far less likely to be tampered with, and the critical data is much less likely to be reused or stolen.

Secure Booting

If you are worried about rootkits and any other low level malware; don't. In this operating system, Windows 10 offers an impossible machine for hackers to break into thanks to the secure booting.

Windows Vista had inaugurated the secure booting. It had used BitLocker and TPM chip in order to protect the booting process. Windows 7 then debuted Unified Extensible Firmware Interface, which had replaced the highly vulnerable traditional BIOS, and then Windows 8 had incorporated the secure boot protections by adding in the newer UEFI version. Windows and UEFI work together in order to make sure that the hardware and the lowest levels of the operating system are not tampered with. If there should be any tampering, you will get a warning or an unauthorized modification is prevented.

Debuting in the Windows 8, a feature that is called Windows Trusted Boot offers code integrity validation that offered protections for all of the Windows boot function from any tampering and automatically remediates if the tampering is found. In addition, it also included an early launch anti malware capability, which had ensured the antimalware software began before the malware could launch. In the previous versions of Microsoft's Windows, malware could begin before the AV and was able to tamper with the functions. However, you still needed to ensure that the preferred anti malware software had supported ELAM.

Windows Hello

Windows Hello is an attempt to get rid of the passwords, which is often wimes stolen and also reused. Hello supports three different methods of biometric authentication, which is the fingerprint, face, and iris; in concert with a PIN.

Many devices and computers that are purchased today support Windows Hello, and the devices that detect the biometric identifiers has been tested to make sure that they cannot easily be hacked. Microsoft worked hard with the members of the Chaos Computing Club, which had experienced hacking biometric devices.

Hello is only for logons. The stored information will never leave the device, and even is an attacker takes it, it would just be useless on any other device. Once you are successfully authenticated using this software, the newer Passport authentication mechanism can be used.

Passport

Microsoft Passport is a single sign on solution that is advanced and has little to do with the option from a year ago. Behind the scenes, this software supports the open FIDO Alliance and it works with a public key cryptography, although you do not need PKI in order to use it. From the behind the scenes technical perspective, it actually works like a smart card, but it does not need a separate card or a card reader.

If the computer has a TPM chip, the private key of your asymmetric key pair is also securely stored there instead of being inside the software. You use the PIN or Hello in order to authenticate locally, then you will use Passport in order to securely authenticate to a different network location. Passport also works with the enterprise Active Directory, Microsoft account, Azure
Active Directory, or any other FIDO identity provider.

Credential Guard

If you are worried about the pass the hash attacks, then you will need to implement the Credential Guard. It will protect the authentication broker and the user's derived credentials in the VBS. This is done by isolating the authentication service, as well as protecting the NTLM credential data.

On the downside, this does not protect the local credentials, which are located in the registry or on the local disk. It does not currently work with the Remote Desktop Protocol logons. However, if you ensure that the local administrative passwords are unique between the computers, then the typical password attacker will be slowed or stopped.

Device Guard

Device Guard is a highly secure tool that will determine which of the applications and scripts should be able to run on a certain computer. Windows had had a close feature since the Windows XP operating system, which has since improved with AppLocker. However, Device Guard uses hardware power in order to protect the integrity of what is and is not allowed to run on the computer. Companies and even vendors are able to add the approved software to the list of the applications that are allowed to run. If used properly, it can even prevent most of the maliciousness from happening. Microsoft also recommends that you use Device Guard, as well as AppLocker.

Enterprise Data Protection

BitLocker protects the data when the device is stolen or lost, however, how do you protect it from those users who may accidentally leak the data? This is where a feature of Windows 10 comes in. It is called Enterprise Data Protection. It provides persistent file level encryption and the basic rights management to corporate the files.

Enterprise Data Protection does not get in any way of the experience using the computer. You are able to continue to use the apps that you like or even choose access protected content. Those users that are not required to work with the special folders, move into secure partitions or zones, or change modes. Windows acts like a broker that gates the user and the app access to a protected data based policy that you have defined.

Enterprise Data Protection is an amazing program that identifies, protects, and separates data. In many cases it is able to do so without any need for app wrapping or reengineering. EDP can be used in combination with the Rights Management and Azure Active Directory services to offer secure B to B sharing.

Miscellaneous Features

There are so many tiny changes that actually make a Windows 10 computer more or easier to secure. For example, DMA Attack Mitigation, the EMET enabled protections, and the ability to prevent local accounts from logging on over a network. Also, do not forget that the security options that are available in other versions of Windows include Account Control, Kerberos Armoring, TPM Key Attestation, SmartScreen, Advance Auditing, and so much more.

Chapter 12: Choosing the Best Anti-Virus

Consumer antivirus programs or software is much like purchasing an insurance policy. It is arguably the most crucial program that you will install on your computer, yet it is often the very last program a user ever wants to purchase or use. Another similar feature between the insurance and the antivirus software is what is also called a risk.

Nowadays, no matter if it is free, expensive, built in, or compare, the best antivirus program will depend on the level of risk that the user will undergo. Those that are really at risk might feel a bit more comfortable with a top shelf, higher priced program, whereas the person who has less concern may just want to download a free program.

Although Windows 10 offers an antivirus, which is called Windows Defender, the fact of the matter is there are many people who want another anti-virus.

- If you absolutely want the best protection: You are going to have to pay more. Kaspersky is a highly ranked program that has passed various different antivirus tests, and the interface is very user friendly.
- If you need the best free protection: You are able to examine the ranking on your own in order to

see the best of the free options; however, Avira Free Antivirus offers the best balance between the non instructions and the protection. It normally scores pretty high for protection.

- If you would like the least intrusive of the free protection options: Windows Defender will not trick you into installing something that you do not want. It will never nag with any ads. If you care about intrusiveness more than you do about the protection, Windows Defender is a good option. Windows Defender automatically disables itself when you install another third party antivirus. It will re-enable again if you uninstall that antivirus. It is designed to get out of your way, yet not leave you vulnerable.

Having an antivirus is pretty important; however, these days it is more important that you use a good program to protect the web browser and the plug ins, which are the biggest targets for attackers now. MalwareBytes Anti-Exploit is a free program that is highly recommended. It functions very similar to the EMET security tool, but it is more friendly to the user and it offers more security features. This will help block common exploit techniques.

While you are getting and installing protective software, it is recommended to download MalwareBytes Anti-Malware. It is a good and solid anti-malware program that functions great with an antivirus and an anti-exploit program. It will find a lot the junkware that is typically forgotten by the antivirus.

Those who would like a specific Antivirus for Windows and need a free option, you need to download Avira. It is free and is specifically created for Window operating machines. Here is a list of the features that you get with this free program:

- Scanning detects the threats in real time from the files as you are using them.
- Starts a full system scan on your demand.
- Schedules updates and scans when you would like.
- You can manage the firewall setting right in Avira.
- You are able to view event logs in order to help analyze any threats.
- It has won awards for the real world protection, overall performance, file detection, as well as malware removal.

This program is tested rigorously every year. It has stood out in many key areas. I has received awards in different areas, overall, it has been set forward and the number one free app for security. Avira had also taken home awards from the AV Test in the year 2015. It received the top ranking spot for usability for two years in a row, and now has also won for the best repair tool, even over Malwarebytes.

Avira earns the usability awards as well. While it is not quite set and forget it programs, it is very close. After you have installed it, Avira will set to run a system scan every seven days. The real time feature will be active too. If you would like to perform or even schedule a full scan you will need to do it manually. It is a great idea to run at least one deep scan as soon as you open the program for the first time.

Chapter 13: Windows 10 and Your Printer

In this chapter you are going to learn how to get your printer to work with your computer that is now running Windows 10. Most printers that are connected to computers are using a USB port and they often work just by plugging them in. A new printer can also come with specific driver that is located on a disc. Here is how you will add your printer to your computer:

- You will sign in on your computer through the administrator account.
- Connect the printing device to your computer.
- Click on the Start button on the desktop screen.
- From there you will click on Settings.
- In the Settings window, you will click on Devices.
- Once this window is open, on the left pane, ensure that the select the category Printers & Scanners.
- From the right, under the Add Printers and Scanners section, you will click on Add a Printer or Scanner.
- You will wait while the computer searched for the printer that is connected. If the computer finds your printer, you are able to click on the name and then follow the instructions on the screen in order to finish the installation process.

If the computer fails to detect your printer, then you will continue with the steps.

- If the computer can't detect the printer, click on the printer that I want is not listed.
- On the option Find a printer with other options, click on the Add a local printer or network printer with manual settings button.
- Click on the Next button.
- On the window Choose a printer port, leave the default options chosen, and then click on the Next button. If you are advanced, you can also just choose a different option from the drop down list; Use an existing port.
- On the window Install the Printer Driver, from your displayed list of manufacturers of printers, click in order to select the one that you have connected to your computer.
- From the right side, locate your model and click it.
- Click on the next button.
- Continue through selecting your correct options.
- Type in the name of the printer and then click on the next button.
- On the window Printer Sharing, ensure that the Share This Printer so that other... button is selected. Continue on until you get to finish.

Conclusion:

Windows 10 is a modern style of a classic operating system that has made its home inside of yours. It is a household name, brand, and system. From the beginning all the way to this upgraded "Perfect 10", this system has a lot to offer from features to style. Learn what this system has to offer and you will be able to keep sensitive information safe and add functionality, along with organization into your life. From the special security features all the way to the ease of use, you will surely fall in love with Windows Thank you again for downloading this book!

I hope this book was able to help you find better sense of windows 10

Finally, if you enjoyed this book, then I'd like to ask you for a favor, would you be kind enough to leave a review for this book on Amazon? It'd be greatly appreciated! Thank you and good luck!

www.ingramcontent.com/pod-product-compliance
Lightning Source LLC
Chambersburg PA
CBHW061041050326
40689CB00012B/2929